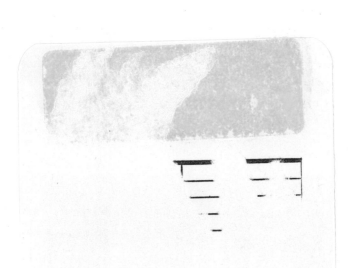

GREAT
MISTAKES

GREAT
MISTAKES

DANIEL COHEN

ILLUSTRATIONS BY
MARGARET C. BRIER

M. Evans and Co., Inc.
New York

Library of Congress Cataloging in Publication Data

Cohen, Daniel.
  Great mistakes.

  Bibliography: p.
  Includes index.
  SUMMARY: Describes some of the great mistakes throughout history in such fields as politics, sports, and architecture.
    1. History—Errors, inventions, etc.—Juvenile literature.
  [1. History—Errors, inventions, etc.]

  I. Title.
  D10.C63   909   79-18036
  ISBN 0-87131-306-5

M. Evans and Company, Inc.
216 East 49 Street
New York, New York 10017

Design by Robert Bull

Manufactured in the United States of America

9 8 7 6 5 4 3 2 1

To Elizabeth and the Flying Scotsman

CONTENTS

GREAT
MISTAKES

WE ALL MAKE MISTAKES

"**I** don't make many mistakes," said New York's colorful mayor Fiorello La Guardia. "But when I make one it's a beaut."

La Guardia was commenting on the discovery that one of the men he had appointed to office was a crook.

Of course La Guardia made mistakes. So do other mayors, and presidents, kings, generals, policemen, judges, scientists, explorers, millionaires, baseball players, parents, and students. We all make mistakes, lots of them. As you will see, it is those people who think that they can't make mistakes who often make the worst ones.

This is a book about history's more famous mistakes. Some of these mistakes are foolish or funny. Others are serious, terrifying, or disastrous.

The handful of stories in this book in no way covers all of the great mistakes of history. There are hundreds, even thousands of other errors that might have been included.

The aim of this book—aside from providing some entertainment—is to show you that when you make a mistake, you are not alone. You are in the company of some of the most powerful and smartest people in history.

11

THE $25,000 "ONION"

The country of Holland is famous for its tulips. Every spring hundreds of thousands of tourists crowd into Holland for the tulip festival. Public parks and private gardens are covered with a huge variety of the brightly colored flowers.

In America wherever there are a large number

of people of Dutch origin tulips are sure to be found. The city of Holland, Michigan, holds a major tulip festival every year.

There is no doubt that the Dutch love their tulips. But a little over three hundred years ago the Dutch didn't just love tulips—they went absolutely crazy over them.

The whole tulip madness started slowly. The tulip is not native to Holland. The flower first became popular in Turkey. In fact the name *tulip* may come from the Turkish word for turban. Wealthy Turks prided themselves on their collections of tulips. European visitors to Turkey were attracted by the flower. They began taking tulip bulbs back with them so that they could grow the flower in their own gardens and greenhouses. Rich Europeans liked to collect strange and exotic plants and animals. To them the tulip seemed very exotic.

In its natural state the tulip is a fairly sturdy flower. It also isn't very pretty. In gardens and greenhouses, however, the tulip can be changed. Tulips of an amazing variety of colors and shapes can be produced.

The trouble is, the more beautiful or exotic the tulip becomes, the harder it is to grow. But people are strange. Often the more trouble a thing gives them the more attached to it they become. The smallest or most sickly puppy or kitten in a litter usually becomes the favorite. So it was with tulips. The mere fact that tulips were hard to grow made them seem more valuable.

Tulip growing became popular throughout Europe during the late 1500s. Nowhere in Europe were the flowers more popular than in Holland. First tulips appeared only in the gardens of the rich. Then middle-class people picked up the tulip-growing habit. Finally, no one in Holland could be considered respectable unless he had a tulip collection. The rarer and more expensive the flowers, the better their owner was thought of. Many people spent far more than they could really afford on buying tulip bulbs.

Year after year the price of tulips rose steadily. Then in 1634 something happened. People stopped buying tulip bulbs simply for display. They began to think they could make a lot of money very quickly by buying and selling tulips. Since the price of tulip bulbs always seemed to go up, people began buying bulbs, hoping to sell them at a higher price a few months later. The more people who bought the bulbs, the higher the price went. The higher the price went, the more people thought they could make money on tulips, and so on. Some people did make a lot of money. But the price rise could not go on forever.

Still, for three years Holland was in the grip of a genuine tulip-mania. The price of tulip bulbs skyrocketed. People invested all of their savings and mortgaged their homes and businesses just to buy a few tulip bulbs. At the height of the mania the price of a single bulb of a rare variety of tulip had reached $40,000 or $50,000.

The mania developed so quickly that a person who had been away from Holland for a few years

would have had no idea what had happened. That was the case with a Dutch sailor. He had been on a long voyage to the Middle East. He knew nothing of tulips, and cared less. But he returned to his homeland right in the middle of the tulip-mania.

When his ship docked, the sailor was sent to the warehouse of the ship's owner, a wealthy merchant. It was the sailor's duty to tell the merchant that his ship and cargo had arrived safely. Since ships on long voyages were often lost in those days, this was happy news for the merchant. As a reward for bringing such good news the merchant presented the sailor with a fine red herring for his lunch.

The sailor was delighted with the herring. Still he felt that a herring alone was not enough for lunch. He wanted something to go along with the herring. Something like an onion. The sailor looked around. The warehouse was crammed with goods of every description.

On the counter the sailor saw what he took to be a small onion. The perfect thing to finish off his lunch, he thought. Surely no one would notice, or mind the the loss of such a humble and common item. So when no one was looking he slipped the "onion" into his pocket and walked to the dock to eat his lunch.

Tulip bulbs look very much like small onions. This one happened to be a bulb for a rare variety known as the Emperor Augustus. It was worth about $25,000. The bulb was the most expensive single item in the entire warehouse.

When the merchant discovered that the tulip

bulb was missing he was horrified. He proceeded to turn the warehouse upside down looking for it. Then he remembered the sailor. Thinking the sailor must have stolen the bulb, the merchant and his employees set out to find him. Their task was an easy one. The sailor had not tried to hide. They found him sitting on the dock, chewing up the last of his lunch. When the sailor, quite innocently, described how he had eaten the valuable tulip bulb, the merchant nearly collapsed.

The poor sailor paid for his lunch, and his ignorance. The merchant brought charges against him, and he was sent to jail for several months.

There is another story from that period that seems scarcely less incredible. It is about an English visitor to Holland. The visitor was an amateur botanist. On a visit to the greenhouse of a wealthy Dutchman he spied a strange-looking "onion." Being interested in unusual plants the Englishman took out his penknife and cut the "onion" up to see what it looked like on the inside. When his Dutch host saw what was going on he exploded in a rage.

"Do you know what you are doing?" he screamed.

"Peeling a most unusual onion," the Englishman replied.

"Don't you know it's an Admiral van der Eyck."

"Thank you," said the visitor, taking out his notebook to write down the name. "Are these admirals common in your country?"

"Death and the Devil," screamed the Dutchman. He grabbed the English visitor by the collar and hauled him off to jail. The Englishman had to stay in jail until he could send for $40,000, the value of the Admiral van der Eyck bulb he destroyed.

The tulip-mania could not last forever, and it didn't. By 1637 the bottom had dropped out of the tulip market. A bulb that had sold for $40,000 at the height of the mania could be bought for $400 or less a few months later. And the price kept right on dropping.

What had happened? The tulip had not suddenly become less beautiful or easier to grow. It was that people realized that tulip bulb prices could not rise forever. At some point they would have to come down. People who had large stocks of expensive bulbs decided to sell out before the price dropped. Once a few started selling and the price went down a bit, people got scared and everybody started to sell. It was the exact reverse of the sort of mania that had driven the price up in the first place. Now, instead of fortunes being made, fortunes were being lost.

After it was over, there were a lot of wiser and poorer people in Holland. And there was one ordinary sailor who may have eaten the most expensive lunch in history.

AN IMPERIAL
MISUNDERSTANDING

If we knew what was going to happen in the future, we would make fewer mistakes in the present. For that reason mankind has spent an awful lot of time and effort to foretell the future.

An unbelievable number of methods for seeing the future have been tried. People have tried to interpret dreams. They have looked at the stars and at tea leaves left in the bottom of a cup. There are those who have claimed that they can read the future by gazing into a crystal ball or turning over playing cards.

Today one can still find a fortuneteller in many places. Astrology columns and magazines that are supposed to predict the future by the stars are extremely popular. People who say they have "psychic" powers and can predict the future get a lot of attention in some newspapers and magazines.

Still modern attempts to foretell the future are not usually taken too seriously. Even people who read the daily astrology column rarely allow their lives to be ruled by what they read. Predictions are rarely very exact. People can usually make of them whatever they wish. Most people work things out so that they think that the prediction advised them to do what they wanted to do anyway.

People have always been that way. Even in ancient times when people believed in predictions more deeply than they do today, they would make the prediction fit their desires.

There was a Greek commander whose ships were attacking a harbor town. The attack was not going well. The Greek supplies were running low. The commander had a choice, should he give up the battle and withdraw, or risk everything on a final attack?

Whenever the Greeks went off to war they took with them a special individual known as an augur. It was the task of the augur to interpret certain signs

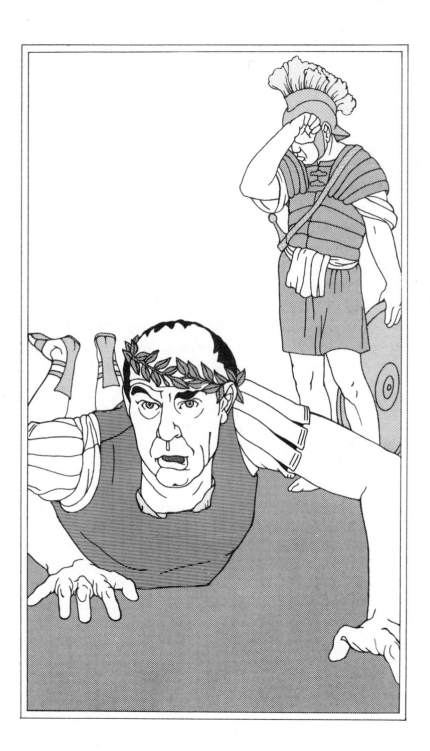

or omens. The omens were supposed to give a clue to what would happen. The augur brought out the sacred chickens. Grain was sprinkled in front of the chickens. If the chickens ate the grain, it would be a sign to withdraw. If they did not eat the grain, it would be a sign to attack.

The sacred chickens did not eat. The commander, who wanted to withdraw, became enraged. "If they will not eat, then they will drink," he shouted, and threw the chickens overboard into the sea. Then, so the story goes, he did withdraw and his ships were destroyed in a storm.

The Roman leader Julius Caesar was about as unsuperstitious a person as has ever lived. He did not believe in prophecies, signs, or omens. But he knew that his soldiers did believe in such things. If the omens for victory were favorable before a battle, then the soldiers would fight harder. They believed they were assured of victory. If the omens were not favorable, then they would become discouraged. They might think that there was little use in fighting, since they were going to lose anyway.

At one point Caesar led his armies to Africa. He knew that there would be many hard battles ahead. As Caesar stepped off the ship to set foot on Africa for the first time, he tripped and fell flat on his face. The soldiers who were watching their commander's arrival gasped. This seemed to be a very bad omen. It was a sign that Caesar's plan, like Caesar himself, would fall in Africa.

Caesar was a master at taking advantage of

situations. He knew what his men were thinking. So instead of just getting up, he lay on the ground and shouted, "Africa I embrace you." There was a moment of silence, then all the men cheered. Caesar had turned the omen around. Instead of looking as if he had fallen, Caesar made it appear as if he had taken all Africa in his arms.

The most famous of all prophecy stories concerns King Croesus of Lydia and the Oracle at Delphi. An oracle is a place where prophecies are supposed to be given. The word is also used to describe the prophecy itself. Delphi is a place in Greece. Since very ancient times it was a place said to be favored by the god Apollo. At Delphi the god was supposed to give out prophecies or oracles.

There was a great temple or shrine at Delphi. In the center of the temple was a cave. In the center of the cave sat the high priestess of Delphi. People would send questions to Delphi. If they gave a rich enough gift to the shrine, then the question would be given to the priestess. The priestess would then go into a trance and deliver an answer. The trouble was, the priestess's answer was usually gibberish. No one could understand what her words meant. Her words had to be interpreted by other officials at Delphi. Even then the answer was never very clear, or didn't make much sense. People talked of a Delphic answer, that is, an answer that no one could really understand.

But that didn't stop people from going to Delphi. For hundreds of years kings, princes, generals, and merchants showered the shrine with gifts in order to have questions answered. There was some suspicion that many of the gifts were really little more than bribes. People didn't just want answers from the Oracle, they wanted favorable answers.

The Oracle was popular not only with the Greeks. Questions and gifts came in from all over the world. Perhaps the most lavish patron the Oracle ever had was King Croesus of Lydia. Croesus ruled a large and extremely wealthy kingdom. In fact, even today there is a saying "rich as Croesus," meaning a person is rich indeed.

For years Lydian gold poured into Delphi. Croesus also sent the Oracle questions from time to time. Like all kings, Croesus had many problems in which knowledge of the future would be helpful. One of his problems was Persia. The Persians had begun to build a large empire. Their influence was expanding into lands near those controlled by Croesus. The border between Croesus' lands and those of the Persians was the River Halys. Croesus not only wanted to stop Persian expansion, but also wanted to take over the Persian empire. So he asked the Oracle what would happen if his armies crossed the River Halys.

The reply Croesus received was that if he crossed the River Halys, "A great empire would fall." It was a typical Delphic answer. But since Croesus wanted to attack the Persians anyway, he decided that he had been given a favorable answer.

Croesus' army crossed the River Halys in 546 B.C. The Lydians were completely defeated by the

Persians under their great king Cyrus. As a result Croesus' empire collapsed and he became a prisoner of Cyrus.

Croesus thought the Oracle had misled him. He sent a messenger to Delphi demanding to know why, after all the gifts he had sent to the Oracle, he had been given the wrong answer. The Oracle is said to have replied that the answer was perfectly correct, but that Croesus had not bothered to ask which empire would fall.

THE WRONG MAN

There is an old legend that everyone has a perfect double. The story isn't true, but there are people who look a lot like one another. This has led to some terrible legal mistakes.

The classic mistake is the case of Adolph Beck. In December 1896 Beck was walking down Victoria

Street in London. Suddenly a woman he had never seen before rushed up to him. She was very angry. She demanded that Beck give her back her watches and rings. Beck didn't know what she was talking about, and told her so. But she would not stop. She grew angrier and angrier and her complaints grew louder and louder, attracting a crowd.

Beck decided that the only way to get rid of this madwoman was to go to the police. So he found the nearest policeman and complained that a strange woman was bothering him. The policeman listened to Beck, and to the woman. Then to settle matters he took both of them to the Rochester Row police station.

Beck was sure that a talk with the police would settle matters. But events took a nightmarish turn for Adolph Beck. He was ultimately sentenced to seven years in prison, and actually served five, for another man's crimes. To make matters worse, three years after his release Beck was again arrested for this man's crimes. Again he was found guilty and nearly sent back to prison. But this time luck was with him. The police realized that they had the wrong man, because they had finally captured the right one.

Here is what happened. The woman who had accused Beck on the street was named Ottiline Meissonnier. She was a teacher of languages. A few weeks before she accosted Beck she had been walking down Victoria Street.

A well-dressed and very polite man tipped his hat to her and asked her if she was Lady Everton.

Ottiline said she was not, but the man struck up a conversation. Ottiline was charmed by his politeness and by his apparent wealth. He talked casually of his huge estate and of the many servants he employed. So Ottiline invited him to tea.

When they met again the man nearly swept Ottiline off her feet. He told her that he was the cousin of Lord Salisbury, at that time the prime minister of Great Britain. He also said that he found her to be such charming and delightful company that he wished to take her to the French Riviera on his yacht. Ottiline was overjoyed at the thought.

Then "Lord Salisbury's cousin" said that proper clothes would be needed for the trip. A teacher of languages didn't have the money to buy fancy clothes. The man waved aside such petty problems. He was rich, he said, and could pay for whatever was needed. He wrote out a check for a substantial sum of money and told Ottiline to go and buy whatever clothes she needed.

There was also the matter of jewelry. Ottiline owned two jeweled watches and some rings of moderate value. The man said these would be not quite right for the trip. The man took the watches and rings saying he would replace them with more fashionable and valuable ones.

The man who called himself Lord Salisbury's cousin was a crook. His whole story was a con game aimed at stealing her watches and rings. A few hours later when she tried to cash the check she had been

given, Ottiline found out she had been tricked. The check was worthless.

She went to the police. They had heard the same story from other women. A man who called himself Lord Wilton and Lord Willoughby had pulled exactly the same trick many times, with remarkable success. It was one of the oldest and simplest confidence games known.

Since the man had gotten cleanly away, there was nothing Ottiline or the police could do. Then came that day in December when she thought she saw "Lord Salisbury's cousin" again, on the very street where he had first tipped his hat to her. This man turned out to be the unfortunate Adolph Beck.

Now Beck was no saint. He had lived in different parts of the world, supporting himself as best he could. His life was erratic but not criminal. Unfortunately, he had few friends, and no one who could swear to where he had been on any particular day.

Other women who had been cheated by the phony lord were called in by the police. They all identified Beck as the man who had swindled them.

Then the police recalled that several years earlier a man named John Smith had been arrested for similar frauds. The two officers who had arrested John Smith were called in. They both said that Beck was the man they had arrested.

A handwriting expert was consulted. He compared Beck's handwriting with samples of John Smith's handwriting. They were not at all alike. But the expert had a simple explanation for that. Beck had been disguising his handwriting.

When Beck was brought to trial there was another terrible coincidence. The judge he faced was the same man who had sentenced John Smith to jail years earlier. The judge was sure that John Smith stood in front of him again. Beck protested as strongly as he could, but it was no use. He was convicted and sent to prison. In prison he was even given John Smith's old prison number. As far as the law was concerned Adolph Beck was John Smith.

Three years after he was released from prison, Adolph Beck was again in trouble. A young woman accused him of stealing money and jewelry from her. The trial was brief, and Beck was again found guilty.

But while awaiting sentence, Adolph Beck's incredible string of bad luck finally changed. The police arrested another man for pulling the same kind of swindles that Beck had been accused of. The man's name was William Thomas. To Detective Inspector Kane it seemed odd that two swindlers should be using exactly the same technique. So he went to see Thomas. Kane immediately saw that Thomas looked very much like Beck.

After that it was not hard to discover that Thomas had committed all of the swindles that Beck had been accused of. Beck was freed and given £5,000 (about $25,000) compensation. It was a fair amount of money in those days, but not much at all considering how much trouble this case of mistaken identity had caused Adolph Beck.

THE UNSINKABLE SHIP

It is always a mistake to believe your own publicity. Just this sort of mistake caused the greatest ocean liner disaster in history—the sinking of the *Titanic*.

In 1912 the *Titanic* was the newest, largest, and most luxurious ocean liner in the world. The *Titanic* was to be the proudest addition to Britain's White Star Fleet. Long before the ship sailed there was a great deal of publicity about it.

The owners of the *Titanic* boasted that it was going to set a speed record for crossing the Atlantic. They also said that the ship was so well built that it was "unsinkable."

The *Titanic* was built with a double-bottomed hull. The hull was also divided into sixteen separate watertight compartments. Four of these compartments could be completely flooded without endangering the ship. That is why the *Titanic* was considered unsinkable. No one imagined that more than four compartments could ever be flooded.

The *Titanic* was to make its first crossing of the Atlantic in April 1912. When the big ship left the port of Southhampton in England it carried 1,290 passengers and a crew of 903. The voyage began well. The *Titanic* was steaming its way across the ocean at a high rate of speed. It was going so fast that it seemed certain to set a new crossing record.

The disaster occurred when the ship was a little more than halfway through its voyage to New York. The *Titanic* was about ninety-five miles south of the area of the sea known as the Grand Banks of Newfoundland. Just before midnight on Monday, April 15, 1912, the ship's lookout spotted an iceberg. The iceberg was less than a quarter of a mile away. There was no time to stop or swerve. The *Titanic* struck the iceberg full force.

Hitting the iceberg did not make a loud noise or

create a big jolt on the ship. Most of the passengers were not aware of what had happened. Even those who knew the ship had struck an iceberg were not very alarmed. They didn't think the accident was serious. Some of the more curious passengers came on deck to look at the iceberg. A few leaned over the rail and tried to touch it.

But the captain and the crew were not so calm. They knew how badly the ship had been damaged. The iceberg had ripped a three hundred-foot gash in the *Titanic*'s right side. That was enough to break five of the watertight compartments. The ship was only designed to survive the breakage of four compartments. This was too much, and the *Titanic* began to sink.

The ship's captain, E. J. Smith, asked that all passengers assemble on deck. At first everyone was calm, the accident didn't seem too bad. The captain told the people what had happened. He then said that a decision had been made to abandon ship.

The chief officer of the ship then shouted, "Crews to the boats! Women and children first." Only then did the real seriousness of the situation hit most of the passengers. Not only was the *Titanic* sinking, but there were not going to be enough lifeboats to save eveyone. In fact, while there were over two thousand people on the ship, there were only lifeboat spaces for fewer than one thousand.

Panic broke out aboard the ship. Many women, unwilling to leave their husbands, had to be forced aboard lifeboats. There were also stories of men dress-

ing up as women to get aboard the boats. Survivors told stories of great heroism and great cowardice.

By 2 A.M. all the lifeboats were in the water. The crews had to row furiously to keep their tiny boats from being swamped by waves created by the sinking ocean liner. From their lifeboats the survivors could see the giant ship break in two. They watched both sections slip rapidly beneath the waves. Some said that they could still hear the ship's orchestra playing hymns before it finally disappeared forever.

Another British ship, the *Carpathia,* arrived about 4 A.M. to pick up survivors from the icy waters. The *Carpathia* was responding to the *Titanic*'s distress call. If it had not come so quickly, many more would have died. There were ships closer to the scene of the disaster than the *Carpathia.* They did not pick up the *Titanic*'s distress call because they had no radio operator on duty at that time of night.

At first the world did not realize the size of the tragedy. Only after the *Carpathia* reached New York and the survivors were counted did the horrible truth hit home. Over 1,400 passengers and crewmen had gone down with the *Titanic.* The liner itself, which had cost $8 million to build, was at the bottom of the sea. Even today no one knows the worth of the passengers' personal possessions that sank with the ship.

Why did this terrible tragedy happen? Obviously the ship sank because it hit an iceberg. But why did it hit an iceberg? The night was cold but clear, and visibility was good. Icebergs were common enough in that part of the sea. The captain was experienced and must have been aware of the potential danger. Yet he did not order the ship to slow down when it entered water that might contain icebergs.

A detailed inquiry into the disaster was held. The investigators decided that the ship had been going too fast for conditions. If the *Titanic* had been going more slowly, the iceberg would have been spotted sooner. It could easily have been avoided. At the very least the *Titanic* would not have hit the iceberg at full speed, and the damage would not have been as great.

No one can know what was in Captain E. J. Smith's mind. In the tradition of the sea he went down with his ship. But it is safe to guess that setting a transatlantic speed record was very important to him. He seems to have ignored possible danger because he believed that his ship was unsinkable.

And why were there not enough lifeboats on the *Titanic*? Who needs lifeboats on an unsinkable ship?

THE MONGOOSE
MISTAKE

European settlers brought sugar cane to the island of Jamaica. They also brought the black rat. The black rat wasn't deliberately brought to the island, or anywhere else for that matter. It just came along as a stowaway on ships. For centuries the rat has been one of the sailor's most constant and most unwelcome companions.

The rats loved Jamaica and they loved the sugar cane. By 1870 rats were destroying as much as one-fifth of the island's sugar crop. Plantation owners were desperate to get rid of the rodents. One planter paid a penny for every dead rat he was brought. He paid out over 20,000 pennies before he realized that the rats were breeding faster than they could be killed.

Some plantation owners tried to bring in animals that would kill rats. A man named Thomas Raffle brought in large and very mean ants. These ants did kill some baby rats, but not very many. The ants themselves became first-class pests.

Another plantation owner, Anthony Davis, brought in giant toads. The toads ate the ants and a few rats, but they didn't solve either problem.

Finally in 1872 W. B. Espeut thought he had found the perfect rat-killer—the mongoose.

The mongoose comes from India. It looks like a weasel and is quite common. An adult mongoose is about a foot long. Its bushy tail adds another ten inches. It has a slender body, short legs, and a pointed nose. Most of all a mongoose is extremely fast.

The mongoose is best known for killing snakes. A mongoose can kill a poisonous cobra. It is so fast that it simply gets to the cobra's neck before the cobra has a chance to strike. It is fair to point out, however, that the mongoose doesn't always win. Sometimes a snake will kill a mongoose.

The mongoose does not only eat snakes. It is not particular. It will eat rodents, birds and insects as well as fruits and vegetables. The mongoose is very adaptable. That is why it is so successful.

W. B. Espeut had nine mongooses shipped to him directly from India. He watched hopefully as they rushed off into the rat-infested fields. The mongooses didn't seem to miss the cobras at all. They set right to work on the rats. Within six months Espeut's losses from rats were cut in half.

With a nice warm climate and plenty to eat, the mongooses began to breed. A female mongoose can produce two litters a year, with an average of two to a litter.

Other planters heard of Espeut's success. They wanted their own mongooses. Espeut felt he did not have any to spare. So the other planters hired people to trap mongooses and then release them in their own plantations. This helped the mongoose spread rapidly all over the island. The mongoose was so well adapted to the conditions in Jamaica, however, that once it had been introduced it would have spread anyway.

Planters from other islands began asking for the little animal to help deal with their rat problem. Soon the mongoose was shipped to Cuba, Puerto Rico, Barbados, Santa Cruz, and finally to the Hawaiian Islands.

All was not rosy however. While the mongoose reduced the number of rats, it did not get rid of the rats completely. The main reason is that the mongoose hunts during the day, and rats are active at night. Quickly the rat and mongoose population reached a balance. Then the mongoose began looking around for other things to add to its diet.

It was probably the poor people with their little gardens and flocks of chickens that first realized the mongoose was becoming a problem. As the rat population fell, the mongoose began killing and eating chickens. It could also kill young pigs, lambs, kittens, and puppies. The mongoose could and did eat bananas, pineapples, corn, avocados, pears, sweet potatoes, even coconuts.

The mongoose was also killing off a lot of native animals. There were several species of birds nearly wiped out by the mongoose. Several species of harmless or beneficial snakes also became mongoose food. The mongoose was very efficient at eating the eggs of freshwater and sea turtles.

There were other unpleasant surprises. When the mongoose reduced the number of insect-eating birds, the number of insects increased. There was a particularly large increase in blood-sucking ticks, which became serious pests.

In 1890 a commission was appointed to study the problem. The commissioners decided that the evil results of the introduction of the mongoose far outweighed the benefits. The mongoose itself had become the greatest pest on the island.

But what was to be done about it? No one could think of an animal that ate mongooses. Fortunately for the people of Jamaica the problem more or less solved itself. At least the seriousness of the problem was reduced by natural means.

A new balance of nature was established. The number of mongooses decreased, while some of the animals that seemed to be on their way to total extinction were on the increase. The mongoose, however, still remained a problem. And Jamaica still had plenty of rats.

Practically ever other place where the mongoose was transplanted had similar problems. In Puerto Rico the mongoose brought a little something extra, the fatal disease rabies. The island had been rabies-free until the introduction of the mongoose.

For a while there was talk of bringing the mongoose to the western states of the United States. Farmers and ranchers wanted to get rid of gophers. But the U.S. government had learned something from what had happened in Jamaica and elsewhere. Western farmers were prevented from repeating the mongoose mistake.

THE END OF
THE WORLD

The end of the world has been predicted thousands of times. All the predictions have been wrong—so far. Yet end-of-the-world prophets are hard to discourage. And they can always find at least a few followers. Hardly a year goes by that we do not hear of some little group somewhere, that has crawled into

44

a cave or locked itself into a house to await the end. A few weeks or months later they come out, pale and confused. They don't know what went wrong. They were so *sure* the world was going to end. But this does not discourage another group from doing the same thing somewhere else.

Usually these end-of-the-world groups are fairly small. But in the middle of the last century there was a really big end-of-the-world panic in America.

The man who started the panic was an upstate New York farmer named William Miller. Miller was not a well-educated man. But he was a regular Bible reader. Around 1818 Miller became convinced that he had found a hidden meaning in certain Bible passages. The message he thought he found was that the world was going to come to an end in about twenty-five years—that is, about 1843.

William Miller was a humble man. He did not know why he, and he alone, had seen this message, while so many educated men had missed it. Miller spent years rereading the Bible and rechecking his figures. They always came out the same. The world was going to end about 1843.

Miller began to talk about his idea with a few friends. In general, though, no one paid much attention to him. Still he was known as a good man and a serious Bible student. In 1831 he was invited to talk about his ideas at a small church in a neighboring town. The prospect of talking in front of an audience terrified the simple farmer. He had never done anything like that before. But he went. The talk went better than he expected. So well, in fact, that he was invited to come back and give another talk. After that invitations to speak came frequently.

Over the next eight years Miller addressed audiences in churches all over upstate New York and New England. Many who heard him were converted to his ideas. Those people who followed him were called Millerites. They were sure God was going to destroy the world by fire, and only the Millerites would be saved.

Miller's ideas were all very well for small towns and farming communities. But how would they be received in cities where people were more educated? That question was answered in 1839 when Miller gave his first speech in Boston. He made some of his most important converts in Boston.

From that point on Millerism grew quickly. It attracted hundreds of thousands of people. There were large Millerite groups in most of the cities of the Northeast.

As the predicted end of the world grew closer, the Millerites grew more and more active. They held huge outdoor meetings that went on for days. The Millerites got a big boost from the sudden appearance of a comet at the beginning of 1843. Comets were often thought to be signs that something terrible was about to happen.

Now Miller himself never said exactly when the world was going to end. He didn't know. All he knew was that it would be somewhere around 1843. Somehow a rumor got started that the day was to be

April 23, 1843. When that date passed, and the world was still there, many Millerites were disappointed. But they didn't give up. They waited until the end of 1843.

January 1, 1844, dawned on a world that had not ended, and not even changed. Again the Millerites were disappointed. But they remembered that Miller had never set an exact date. He never even said that the world had to end in the year 1843. Calendars had changed a lot since biblical times. Therefore Miller figured that the outside date for the end of the world was March 21, 1844.

When that date passed without anything happening, the Millerite movement faced a real crisis. Many people simply quit. Miller himself was completely puzzled. He was so sure of his calculations. How could he have made a mistake? He told his remaining followers to hold on, that the end could not be long delayed now. Many of them did keep the faith. And as unbelievable as it may seem, after three disappointments they were still able to pick up new converts, lots of them. By the summer of 1844 there were more Millerites than ever before. And they were more fanatic than ever.

Not everyone who heard William Miller's message thought he was right. In fact, many people thought he was crazy and that all those who followed him were fools.

After March 21, 1844, disappointed Millerites came in for a lot of kidding.

"What! Not gone up yet?" one man shouted at a

Millerite. "We thought you'd gone up! Aren't you going up soon? Wife didn't go up and leave you behind to burn did she?"

The Millerites bore the kidding bravely. They knew that when the end of the world did come they would be taken up to heaven. All those who were cracking jokes would be left behind to burn. Who would have the last laugh then?

The Millerites were still sure the great and terrible day would come soon—but exactly when, that was the problem. One of the members of the movement did his own calculations. He decided that the world would end on October 22, 1844. As the summer of 1844 wore on, more and more Millerites came to believe in the October 22 date. William Miller himself hung back at first. He was not sure. But on October 6, just two weeks before the new final date, Miller too became converted. He was simply carried along by the enthusiasm of his followers.

Now the Millerite movement, from top to bottom, was fully committed to the idea that the world would come to an end on October 22, 1844. The date could not be refigured this time. There would be no turning back.

The Millerites were supremely confident. They looked forward to the great day. They would be raised up and their scoffing enemies thrown down. The wicked old world would be destroyed, and they would live in a new and better world.

Many Millerites sold everything they had. They paid off all their debts with the money. They did not want to face the end of the world owing anybody anything.

On that final night some of the Millerites put on white robes. These were the robes they were supposed to wear when carried up to heaven. They trooped up to mountain and hilltops. There they would await the end of the world with much singing and shouting.

Others gathered in halls and private homes. They spent what they expected would be their last night on earth praying quietly. And they waited, and waited and waited. When the sun finally came up on the morning of October 23, 1844, on an unchanged world, the Millerites suffered a final crushing disappointment.

The Millerite movement was finished. In baseball a batter gets three strikes and he is out. William Miller and his followers got four strikes. The last one was too much. The movement, which had survived three disappointments, could not survive the fourth.

THE WISE MAN
WHO NEVER WAS

━━━━━━━━━━━━━━━━━━━━━━━━━━━

In the year 1460 a monk wearing a travel-stained cloak appeared in the city of Florence, Italy. The monk was in the pay of Cosimo de Medici. Cosimo was the founder and head of the immensely wealthy and powerful Medici family.

The Medici were bankers and politicians. They

were also cultured and educated people. They loved learning and art. The Medici hired people to go all over the world to collect rare books and works of art. The monk was one of the Medici agents.

He had been traveling throughout Europe collecting rare manuscripts for the Medici. In a monastery in northern Greece the monk stumbled across a great prize. It was a nearly complete copy of the works of Hermes Trismegistus, a famous wise man of ancient Egypt. The monk had, of course, heard of Hermes Trismegistus. But like everyone else he assumed that all copies of his writings had been lost.

The monk bought the manuscript and rushed back to Florence. He knew Cosimo would give him a good reception, and he was not disappointed. When Cosimo looked at the document he practically wept for joy.

Unfortunately, Cosimo could not read the manuscript because it was written in Greek. There were very few people in Italy who could read Greek, particularly the sort of old-fashioned Greek used in this book.

But Cosimo had a solution for that little problem. He had his own staff of Greek translators. At the head of this staff was Marsilio Ficino, the finest translator of ancient Greek outside of Greece itself. At that moment Ficino was just getting ready to translate the complete works of Plato. Plato is generally considered one of the greatest, if not the greatest, philosopher in history.

Cosimo told Ficino to put his Plato work aside. He wanted this new book to be translated first. Cosimo was an old man. He was afraid that if he waited, he

would not get a chance to read the works of the famous Hermes Trismegistus before he died. So Ficino set to work. He produced a translation that was to influence European thought for almost two hundred years.

But it was all a huge historical mistake. Hermes Trismegistus never existed. The writings were old, but not ancient. They were a collection of writings, not the work of a single man. Large portions of the book were so mixed up that they made no sense at all. Yet many of the smartest people in Europe thought they were reading great words of wisdom.

How had such a mistake happened? There were several reasons. The basic mistake was thinking the book was ancient. In the fifteenth century a lot of people believed in ancient wisdom. The older a book, the wiser it was supposed to be. People thought the works of Hermes Trismegistus, or the Hermetic works as they were called, had been written in the time of Moses, or even before. Some thought the Hermetic book was the oldest book in the world. In fact, it was only about twelve hundred years old in 1460.

The works had been written, or really put together, during the second century. They came from the Egyptian city of Alexandria. During the second century Alexandria was a meeting place for people of many different lands. All sorts of ideas were exchanged there.

The Hermetic works were a collection of philosophy, mysticism, and magic, all thrown together in a hodgepodge manner. Then someone said that the whole mess had been written by Hermes Trismegistus. That is a strange name. It means three times as great as Hermes. Hermes was a Greek god. The Egyptians also used the name for their own god of wisdom.

Hermes Trismegistus was supposed to have been a king or wise man of most ancient Egypt.

In the second century it was common for people not to use their own name on books but to attribute them to some ancient and well-known wise man. This was not a deliberate hoax. It was just the way things were done. There were hundreds of books that were attributed to King Solomon.

Scholars of the fifteenth century should have been on guard. But they weren't. All known copies of the Hermetic works had disappeared in Western Europe. They were known only by rumor, or by brief quotes in other books. Over the centuries the missing works of Hermes Trismegistus developed a great reputation, mainly because no one had read them.

If the full text of the Hermetic books had always been available, then people probably would have discovered what was wrong with them much sooner. But by the time they were rediscovered so dramatically they had such a great reputation that no one dared to doubt them.

So long as people continued to believe that the books were extremely ancient they seemed quite marvelous. It looked as though they were filled with accurate predictions. But since the books were nowhere near as ancient as people believed, the predictions were not predictions at all. They were just reports of things that had already happened.

Any educated person who read the Hermetic works carefully should have been able to see they were not the products of ancient Egypt. Yet for many years no one questioned their age.

Then, in the seventeenth century, the Hermetic writings were taken on by an English scholar named Isaac Casaubon. Casaubon had not started out to criticize the Hermetic writings. In fact, he only made a few comments about them in a book he had written on an entirely different subject. But the criticisms he made were so telling, and so obvious, that soon everyone began noticing what was wrong. Within a few years the reputation of this great wise man and his marvelous book was completely destroyed. Today, practically no one has ever heard of Hermes Trismegistus. Yet for two hundred years the name and reputation of Hermes Trismegistus had fooled the best minds in Europe. Or to be more to the point, for two hundred years the best minds in Europe had managed to fool themselves.

EL DORADO

In the year 1537 a Spaniard by the name of Gonzalo Jiménez de Quesada led a group of about two hundred men to a high plateau in what is now the South American country of Colombia. The ragged and starving two hundred were all that remained of an expedition that had started out with seven hundred men.

The expedition had set out months earlier with high hopes. But they had lost their way in the jungles and mountains. In truth, they didn't really know where they were going. Many of the men had died of starvation and disease. Their ranks had been thinned by Indian attacks. Those who tried to desert the expedition perished in the wild. It was all a horrible disaster.

De Quesada's expedition had been looking for a place they called El Dorado. What they didn't know was that in 1537 they found it. But they didn't believe they had found it, and they went on searching.

De Quesada himself lived for another thirty years. He made other searches for El Dorado, all unsuccessful. He died at the age of eighty, still searching. De Quesada never became rich from his search, as he had hoped he would. All he had to leave his closest living relative was his royal grant to look for El Dorado. This relative took up the search and died during one of his expeditions.

A lot of other people searched for El Dorado. And a lot of them died. Uncounted thousands of Indians were slaughtered by seekers of El Dorado. The whole episode was one of the bloodiest and maddest in human history.

But why had de Quesada failed to realize that he found what he was looking for? The reason is simple. He was blinded by greed. He was sure El Dorado was a land that contained a huge store of gold. The real El Dorado that he found contained only about two hundred pounds of the precious metal.

When the Spaniards came to the New World they

found a lot of gold. In 1519 Hernán Cortés overthrew the Aztec Empire of Mexico. The Aztec rulers had collected a great deal of gold.

In 1532 Francisco Pizarro overthrew the much larger and richer Inca Empire of South America. He found huge quantities of gold. All this gold was shipped back to Spain. The gold inflamed the imaginations of other ambitious men. They all thought they could find golden kingdoms in the New World.

In fact, there really wasn't much gold in Central and South America. Cortés and Pizarro had already taken most of what there was. But while there wasn't much gold, there were plenty of rumors. All kinds of tales about golden cities were passed around.

One of the most interesting of these tales was the story of *el hombre dorado*—the golden man. According to this story there was a great and rich kingdom. The land was so rich in gold that the king could afford to cover himself in the metal. Every year, so the story went, the king would cover his body with some sticky material. Then he would be sprinkled with gold dust. All golden and gleaming he would be rowed out to the middle of a sacred lake. Then he would jump in the lake. When he came out of the water all the gold dust had been washed off.

There were many versions of this story. Each one added different details. But all the stories contained an account of *el hombre dorado*. After a while people stopped talking about *el hombre dorado,* and said just El Dorado. El Dorado came to mean not only the king who covered himself with gold, but also the place. To the Spaniards, and others, El Dorado was a golden kingdom, a place of untold wealth.

Unlike many rumors about golden kingdoms, there was some truth in this one. There really was a king who once a year covered himself with gold dust, and jumped into a lake. But what those who heard the tale didn't consider was that it doesn't take much gold dust to cover a man's body. So the place where the El Dorado ceremony was performed did not necessarily have to be rich in gold.

Another problem with the El Dorado story was that it was not specific. It did not tell where this marvelous kingdom was supposed to be. So everyone who heard the story had his own idea. Expeditions blundered out in all directions. They usually resulted in the death of most of the expedition members.

Many of the searchers were convinced that the Indians knew where the golden land was. But they thought the Indians were hiding the information. Indians were often captured and tortured to tell what they knew. Since they knew nothing they could tell nothing. The El Dorado searchers refused to believe them. So the Indians often made up stories. They would say that yes, El Dorado was out there somewhere. Usually they indicated a place that was far away or hard to reach. They hoped that the stories would get the murdering madmen out of their territory.

When de Quesada and the ragged survivors of his expedition stumbled onto the high plateau in Colombia in 1537, they had entered the land of the Chibchas. It was a king of the Chibchas who had performed the El Dorado ceremony. It was from this ceremony that all the wild El Dorado rumors had started. But the Chibchas had no gold of their own. What gold they did possess they got from trading with nearby tribes. What the Chibchas traded for gold was salt. Salt was the only substance they possessed in quantity. Salt was not what the El Dorado searchers were looking for.

By the time de Quesada reached the land of the Chibchas in 1537, they had already given up the El Dorado ceremony. They didn't have enough gold to keep it going. That is why de Quesada refused to believe he had found the fabled land. No, he thought, it must be elsewhere. A few days after de Quesada arrived, another group of El Dorado searchers also made their way to the high plateau. They too refused to believe they had found El Dorado. So the search went on.

Belief in the land of El Dorado was not finally laid to rest until the nineteenth century. That was three hundred years after the legend first began.

STONES FROM
THE SKY

If you stand outside on a dark clear night and look up at the sky for a long time, you will probably see a streak of light. Perhaps several of them. The streak of light is what we call a meteor. Some people call them shooting stars.

They are not stars at all. The light is caused by

something—a piece of rock or metal or some other kind of space debris—burning up in the atmosphere. Usually the debris burns up completely. No part of it ever reaches the surface of the earth. But sometimes, a large piece of debris will not burn up completely. Part of it will hit the earth. For centuries people have been finding pieces of rock and metal that have come from space. These are called meteorites.

For a long time people were not sure where these pieces of rock and metal came from. There were stories about how some of them had fallen from the sky. But there were stories about many things.

About two hundred years ago, when scientists first began to study the problem, most of them did not think that stones fell from the sky. The scientists continued to insist that stones did not fall from the sky even after many people reported that they had actually seen stones fall from the sky to the ground.

The general scientific attitude toward meteorites was well summed up by Thomas Jefferson. Jefferson was not only a political figure. He was interested in everything. He was particularly interested in science, and he knew a lot about it.

There was a heavy fall of meteorites over Weston, Connecticut. Two professors from Yale University said that they actually saw these meteorites fall. When Jefferson heard this story he didn't believe it. He was supposed to have said, "I could more easily believe that two Yankee professors lie, than that stones would fall from heaven."

In his whole life Jefferson wasn't wrong about too much. But he certainly was wrong about this. He wasn't alone in his error. Most scientists reacted the same way.

On May 26, 1751, a very bright meteorite or fireball was seen over southern Germany. It hit the ground and exploded near the town of Angram in Croatia. When the residents went to look at the place where the thing exploded they found two large chunks of iron. The biggest one weighed seventy-one pounds. There were many witnesses. The case was very well known.

Andreas Stutz, who was director of the museum in Vienna, wrote about the Angram Meteorite in 1790. He left no doubt as to what his opinion was. "That the iron had fallen from the sky might have been believed in 1751 even by educated people because of the general lack of knowledge of physics and natural history; but in our time it would be indefensible to consider such fairy tales faintly probable."

In 1791 a hail of meteorites fell on and around the town of Juillac in France. The town's lawyer drew up a very formal-sounding report about what had happened. The report was signed by three hundred citizens of the town. They were all solid and respectable people. They were not the sort to believe in fairy tales. The citizens of Juillac sent their report to Paris, to a group of learned men called the Academy. The Academy was at that time probably the most important and respected scientific group in the world. How did the Academy react? They refused to believe the people of Juillac.

One of the Academy members, Pierre Bertholon de Saint Lazare, wrote: "How sad it is to see a whole municipality trying to verify folk tales. . . . It is pitiful. . . . All the necessary remarks will occur to the reader when he reads this authentic report of an evidently wrong fact, about something which is physically impossible."

What about those flashes of light? Most scientists doubted that they had anything to do with the strange pieces of stone or iron. The light flashes might be caused by burning gas high in the atmosphere. Others said that perhaps the flashes were some form of lightning. At the time no one knew what lightning was either.

Meteorites often look as if they had been burned or melted. The scientists thought they were formed when lightning struck the ground. The lightning would then melt rocks on the ground into the shape of the meteorite. Others wondered if volcanoes might somehow be responsible. Perhaps these melted pieces of stone or iron were thrown out by distant volcanoes.

Not all the world's scientists rejected the stones from the sky idea. Back in 1697 a Swiss naturalist named Johann Scheuchzer first put the theory in print. Nobody paid any attention to him.

Edmund Halley, the British astronomer who first proved that comets orbited the sun, also said that the meteorites must come from space. Very few paid any

attention to him. But then very few paid any attention to his comet theory either, at least until a comet returned to the earth's vicinity just when he had predicted. The comet was named Halley's Comet in his honor. But by that time Edmund Halley was already dead.

Some scientists searched old records to find accounts of stones that fell from the sky. They found plenty of them. For example, on November 16, 1492, a loud thunderlike noise was heard all over the region known as Alsace. Then a stone weighing 260 pounds fell into a field near the village of Ensisheim. It made a hole five feet deep. The stone was taken to King Maximilian I who was staying near Ensisheim at the time. The stone is still in the Ensisheim church.

Other stories were less dramatic, but there were so many of them they had to be taken seriously. Evidence was building up. Still the scientists, particularly in the Paris Academy, resisted. Stones, they said, did not fall from the sky.

Finally something happened that even the most stubborn member of the Paris Academy could not overlook. On April 26, 1803, between two thousand and three thousand stones fell on or near the French town of L'Aigle. The stones weighed between a quarter of a pound to over eighteen pounds. When people went to pick the stones up they were still hot. Before they fell, a bright fireball in the sky had been seen by hundreds of people. There were several loud explosions in the air. Then the stones fell. It was, and still is, one of the most spectacular falls of meteorites ever.

The Academy sent one of its own members from Paris to investigate. The evidence was overwhelming. The scientists finally had to admit the obvious. Stones do fall from the sky.

THE BATTLE OF CRÉCY

On a recent list of the ten worst generals in history, the name of Philip VI appears. This fourteenth-century king of France earned his reputation on the basis of one battle—the battle of Crécy. The battle did not cost him his throne. He continued to rule—badly —for many more years. But it was one of the opening battles in a long and terrible conflict between England and France. This conflict came to be known as the Hundred Years War.

The war began when Edward III, king of England, laid claim to the throne of France. The French did not think his claim was a very good one. But that did not stop Edward from invading France in July 1346.

Philip was slow to react, and the English had some early successes. But France was supposed to have the finest knights in all Europe. Soon Philip began to gather a great army. The French were sure they could easily drive out the invaders.

Edward knew he was badly outnumbered. He was in no hurry to meet the French force head on. Edward gave up his march toward Paris. He started marching back to the coast. Whether he intended to return to England at once, or just wanted to be near the coast in case things went badly, is not clear. In any case, the French caught up with him before he reached the sea.

The English king now knew that he was going to have to fight whether he liked it or not. So he decided to make the best of it. On August 16, 1346, the English forces took up good defensive positions of a hill near the village of Crécy.

The French had a far larger force. They were considered to be the better fighters. The French knights were already discussing what they were going to do after they won. But the French had some problems. They had been marching for days and were tired. King Philip thought it might be better to stop and wait until the next day. But he didn't have firm control over his army. Some of the men stopped, others did not. The result was confusion.

Philip wavered. Unable to stop his army he then decided to pursue the battle. The plan was for a troop of crossbowmen, from the Italian city of Genoa, to lead the battle. They were to get close enough to the English to fire their arrows. This would soften up the English troops for the charge of the mounted knights. The mounted knights were the main strength of the French army.

The Genoese, however, were not anxious to fight. They had been marching all day and were tired. There had been a sudden thunderstorm, and their bows were wet. Now the sun had come out, but was shining right in their eyes. The Genoese quite reasonably pointed out that under these conditions they could not give a very good account of themselves in the battle. Since it was already late in the day they thought it would be best to wait until the following day.

By this time Philip had gotten close enough to the English to be able to see them. The sight of the invaders so enraged the French king that he lost whatever good sense he may have had. He would hear nothing of the Genoese complaints. He ordered an all-out attack.

When the attack started the English felt that they had been given a present. The English archers were well rested, had the sun at their backs, and had managed to keep their weapons dry. Besides, English archers used the longbow not the crossbow. The longbow

had a much greater range. In the hands of the skillful English it was a most effective weapon.

The English showered the front ranks of the French with arrows. The discouraged Genoese simply gave up. They threw down their weapons and ran toward the rear.

King Philip was now beside himself with rage. He shouted, "Slay those rascals who get in our way!" So the French knights began slashing their way forward. They were not killing the English, they were killing their own allies.

Meanwhile, the men at the rear of the French army had no idea what was going on at the front. They were strung out for miles down the roads and over the hills. They just kept pressing forward. At the front the French were now caught between the English, against whom they could make no headway, and other French troops pushing up from the rear. The result was hopeless chaos and confusion.

King Edward was sitting on a windmill on the top of a hill. He was delighted with what he saw. So he ordered his army to advance. The English advanced on foot. The English not only had heavily armed knights, but also foot soldiers armed with pikes and long knives. These common soldiers were despised by the proud French knights. But they were murderously effective at Crécy.

The French knights fought bravely. They were too brave for their own good. Each knight charged forward without a thought for his own life. Nor did he give any thought to what else was happening. The knights just kept piling up at the front where they were cut to pieces by the English bowmen and foot soldiers.

King Philip, who had started the whole disaster with his ill-advised order to charge, had now completely lost control. If he had been able to retreat, he would have saved the bulk of his army. Then the French could have fought another day, under more favorable conditions. But the king either wouldn't or couldn't order a retreat until his army had been practically destroyed.

The battle went on far into the night. King Philip was wounded. Finally he was persuaded that he must at least save himself. With just a few companions he fled to a nearby castle and safety. The king left behind him, dead on the field of Crécy, many of France's greatest knights. English losses were very light.

As a direct result of the battle, the French lost the port of Calais. But the worst damage the French suffered was a loss of morale. It was years before the French gained back the self-confidence to seriously try to throw back the invading English.

THE LEANING TOWER
AND THE BENT
PYRAMID

One of the world's best-known and most beautiful mistakes is the Leaning Tower in the Italian city of Pisa. The Leaning Tower is one of Italy's biggest tourist attractions. Practically everyone has seen a picture or drawing of it at one time or another. It is widely admired for its graceful arches made of striking white and colored marble.

But Italy is full of fine buildings. It isn't the grace of the building that attracts the tourists, it's the tilt. The tilt is extremely obvious. The Leaning Tower is more than seventeen feet from being straight up and down. And it is slowly getting worse year by year.

Of course the lean, which has made the tower so famous, was an accident. The tower was designed to be the bell tower for the cathedral at Pisa and it was supposed to be perfectly straight. Work on the tower was begun in about 1174. The architects were Bonanno of Pisa and William of Innsbruck.

The construction went along quite nicely at first. But then, when the tower was less than half finished, the builders realized they had made a mistake, a big one. The ground on which they were building the tower was soft. One side of the building began sinking into the earth. Construction was stopped because no one knew what to do.

For about a century the bottom part of the Leaning Tower stood there unfinished. It appeared to have finally settled completely. The people of Pisa wanted a bell tower for their cathedral, so a plan to finish the Leaning Tower was worked out. The new architects decided to build some of the upper stories out of line with the others. The aim was to make up for the tilt and bring the top of the tower closer to being straight up and down. Work started again in 1275, but it wasn't until 1350 that the building was finally completed.

In spite of the funny tilt it was a handsome building. It was eight stories tall with graceful arches and

marble columns. The top story, which is smaller than the others, contains the bells. In total the tower is 179 feet high and 52 feet in diameter. An inside stairway of 296 steps leads to an observation platform. The walls at the base are 13 feet thick, and about half that at the top. It was the sort of tower that was built to last.

Unfortunately, the attempts to make up for the tilt didn't really work. The base had not completely settled. The tower continues to lean just a little bit further every year. One day, if nothing is done, the Leaning Tower will lean just a little too far and it will fall over. The tower lean was 15½ feet in 1829 and more than 17 feet by the middle of the twentieth century.

Many modern attempts have been made to stop the growing tilt. No one, least of all the people of Pisa, actually want the tower straightened out, even if that were possible. But they would like to stop the tilt at its present angle. The modern attempts have not been any more successful than those of the fourteenth or fifteenth century. Concrete has been injected into the base in the hope of stabilizing the tower. That didn't work. Traffic in the immediate area of the tower has been banned. It was thought that vibrations from the traffic were hurting the already unstable building. That helped a bit but did not solve the basic problem.

Far more elaborate schemes have been proposed. One that was seriously considered was jacking the entire tower up, building a new concrete foundation underneath it, then setting the tower back down.

Others have said that the Leaning Tower should be taken apart and rebuilt somewhere else, where the ground does not sink.

So far none of these schemes has been adopted. There are drawbacks and dangers to all of them. They might destroy the tower rather than save it. The people of Pisa just keep watching their beloved tower and hoping that it will not lean too far too fast.

In terms of solid, long-lasting constructions, the ancient Egyptians had it over everybody else. The Pyramids of Egypt are by far, the oldest large man-made structures still around. They will probably still be here when the buildings of today or those to be built in the future have crumbled into dust.

There is no doubt that the Pyramids are marvelous constructions. They are so marvelous, in fact, that many people doubt that the Egyptians built them. There are always stories about how the Egyptians were helped by men from outer space, or by some sort of supernatural creatures.

When you mention Egyptian pyramids, many people think only of the Great Pyramid at Giza, near Cairo. At most people think of the three Giza pyramids. But the Egyptians built many pyramids, large and small. And some of these pyramids clearly show that the Egyptians, like the rest of us, made mistakes.

There is, for example, a pyramid at a place called Medyum. It is called the Ruined Pyramid. This pyramid looks like a couple of gigantic blocks piled on top of one another, and all surrounded by a huge

mound of rubble. But it was a pyramid once, or at least that is what it was supposed to be.

The pyramid at Medyum was built very early in Egyptian history, before the construction of the Giza pyramids. It was a time when Egyptian builders were still experimenting with the form. The first pyramid was really just a series of blocks or steps. It is called the Step Pyramid. That pyramid was very successful. It is still around. At Medyum the builders started with the basic step form. But then they decided to fill in the steps and give it the nice smooth pyramid shape with which we are familiar. But that plan didn't work. At some point all the fill-in material simply fell off, leaving a step pyramid surrounded by rubble.

Just when this happened no one can tell. Many archeologists believe that it must have happened during construction. That would have been a real disaster. It seems the project was just abandoned. In any case, that exact kind of construction was never tried again.

Then there is the oddity called the Bent Pyramid. For about two thirds of the way up this pyramid is a perfectly ordinary pyramid shape. Then, abruptly, the angle is changed. The result is a bent or blunted-looking pyramid, far shorter than it would have been if construction had been continued on the original angle.

Why the change of plans? No one knows. We don't even know for which king the pyramid was built. But many archeologists have speculated that the pyramid building was going along just fine, when the king died suddenly. His successor then decided to finish off the pyramid as quickly and as cheaply as possible.

Another theory suggests that the Bent Pyramid may have something to do with the Ruined Pyramid at Medyum. Both were built at around the same time. Perhaps builders were already at work on the Bent Pyramid when the pyramid at Medyum collapsed. They may have become frightened that they too were building their pyramid too tall, or on too sharp an angle. So they changed plans, leaving a distinctly funny-looking pyramid.

Whatever the reasons, both the Bent Pyramid and the Ruined Pyramid prove that those infallible Egyptian builders also made mistakes.

THEY COULD NOT
BE HANGED

For hundreds of years hanging has been one of the most popular forms of execution in the Western world. At best it is a terrible way to die.

By the late eighteenth century most public hangings used a high platform and a long rope. The victim stood over a trapdoor. On a signal the executioner would open the trapdoor. The victim would then fall several feet before being stopped by the rope. The result was a tremendous jolt that would almost always break the victim's neck and kill him. This was called the "long drop into eternity."

The spectacle of such a death is horrible even to think about. Yet at one time huge crowds would come to watch public hangings. It was considered a form of entertainment.

Bad as that type of hanging was, it was less cruel than what had gone before. At one time the hangman didn't use the "long drop." The victim was simply stood on a ladder or a cart. The support under his feet was pulled away, and he was left to dangle there. Sometimes the victim was stood on a bucket. Then the bucket was kicked away. From that comes our expression "to kick the bucket," meaning to die. Death came by slow strangulation. That might take many terrible minutes.

Sometimes the victim's friends would try to shorten his agony. They would pull on his legs. This would bring strangulation more quickly. A quick twist of the dangling body might break the neck. By this method a person was "turned off" in a very real way.

In addition to being extremely painful, the slow strangulation method of hanging was not always a sure thing Even after dangling for fifteen minutes or more, the victim might not actually be dead, but merely unconscious.

Even today, with all our advanced medical knowledge, it is sometimes hard for doctors to decide whether a patient is really dead. It was much harder a few centuries ago. There was talk of "miracle resurrections." That is, persons who had been hanged and were supposed to be dead, but later "came back to life." Of course, they had not really been dead in the first place.

These "miracle resurrections" were not nearly as common as they were said to be. They do make good stories, and everybody loves a good story. But there are at least a few cases where there is a good deal of evidence to show that the executioner made a mistake, and the hanged person did "come back to life."

There was, for example, the case of William Duell. In 1740 Duell was hanged for murder at Tyburn, the place of public execution near London. Duell hung for a few moments, and everyone assumed he was dead. So he was cut down, and his body was placed in a coffin. There was no great rush to get rid of the body. That was very lucky for William Duell. A few hours later someone noticed that the "corpse" was breathing. He was breathing slowly, but he was breathing. A bit later Duell actually sat up and was given a bit of wine to drink. Duell was in great pain, but he was very definitely alive.

There are stories about how "revived" prisoners were hanged a second time. This didn't happen to William Duell. He had been hanged once, and as far as the law was concerned that was enough. But he was not set free. Instead he was sent to the colonies.

One of the most famous cases is that of "Half-

Hangit" Maggie Dickson. She was hanged in the public market in Edinburgh, Scotland, in 1728. After the hanging her relatives cut her down and put her in a coffin. The coffin was placed on a cart. She was to be taken back to her home at Musselburgh, about nine miles from the place where she had been hanged.

The cart bumped over the cobblestone streets. And somewhere along the line the bumping cart shook the unconscious Maggie "back to life." She fully recovered from her hanging. Apparently she was also pardoned for whatever crime it was she had been sentenced to death for in the first place.

Not only did Maggie survive her hanging, but she lived on to be a very old woman. She had a large number of children. She was a real source of pride to her neighbors. Whenever a stranger visited Musselburgh they were told the story of "Half-Hangit" Maggie, and if the old woman happened to be around, she was pointed out to them.

Persons who were executed were not always buried. Often their bodies were turned over to medical schools. There the bodies were cut up, or dissected, for the education of medical students. Condemned criminals had a special horror of being dissected after death. Some were afraid that they would wake up while the medical students were cutting them up. Hanging was bad enough, but being dissected seemed even worse.

There is a record of this actually happening. On February 20, 1587, a murderer was hanged in London. After he was cut down his body was rushed to the

Surgeons Hall. There his chest was cut open by a group studying anatomy. Much to their surprise they discovered that the unfortunate man's heart was still beating. But he managed to survive only for three more days. When he died the second time, he was dead for good.

There is also a story about a group of eighteenth century German doctors who were not so humane. According to this tale they abandoned their job as healers and decided to finish the hangman's work for him.

These doctors were given the body of a notorious murderer who had been hanged. But when the chief surgeon examined the body he discovered faint signs of life.

He told his fellow doctors that he was pretty certain that with proper treatment the "dead" man could be restored to life. Then he said, "But consider what a rascal we should again have among us. He was hanged for a cruel murder. If we restore him to life, he will probably kill somebody else. I say, gentlemen, all these things considered, it is my opinion that we had better proceed in the dissection."

They did.

THE LYING STONES

No one makes bigger mistakes than the person who is sure that he cannot be making a mistake. For example, consider what happened to Dr. Johann Bartholomew Adam Beringer in the 1720s. Dr. Beringer was senior professor and dean of the Faculty of Medicine, doctor of Philosophy and Medicine, and chief physician to the prince-bishop of Würzburg.

That sounds like a very important title. It was not misleading. Dr. Beringer was a very important man. He was not only well respected in Würzburg, but well known throughout Europe. When Dr. Beringer spoke, people listened.

Dr. Beringer had strong opinions on many subjects. One of the subjects in which he was most interested was fossils. Today we know that fossils are the remains of plants and animals that lived long ago. Over the centuries these remains have been turned to stone. But back in the days when Dr. Beringer lived, people were not sure what fossils were.

Some thought that fossils were the remains of living things. Others thought they were not. One of those who thought they were not was Dr. Beringer. He believed that fossils were "sports of nature," ordinary stones that had, for some unknown reason, been shaped like natural objects. It wasn't a very good theory even 250 years ago. But Dr. Beringer was not the only educated person who believed in this theory. However, he was one of the loudest in defending it.

Dr. Beringer had a desire to gather a collection of fossils. In 1725 he hired three young men to dig for fossils in the hills near Würzburg. At first results were poor. Then they dug into one hillside and struck what Beringer called "one bountiful horn of plenty."

The three young men brought Dr. Beringer stones with the likenesses of butterflies, bees, frogs, lizards, fish, and hundreds of other small animals on them. There were also stones with leaves, plants, and flowers upon them.

But that wasn't all. One of the first stones brought to Dr. Beringer showed the sun and its rays. There were also clear pictures of the moon, the stars, and of comets with their tails.

Most amazing of all were the stones with letters on them. Sometimes there was just a single letter. Other times there were entire words in Latin, Hebrew, and even Arabic. Occasionally, Dr. Beringer would be given a stone with a snail or some other creature bearing a letter on its shell.

All in all, over two thousand of these remarkable stones were delivered to the delighted Beringer by his three associates. Now you might think that Dr. Beringer would be just a little suspicious of this fantastic find. A lot of other people thought he was being tricked and said so. But Beringer didn't suspect a trick for a minute.

J. Ignatz Roderick and Georg von Eckart, two learned citizens of Würzburg, attacked Beringer for saying the stones were genuine. They didn't just attack Beringer with words either. They carved a few stones and had them sold to Beringer as genuine. Roderick and Eckart openly admitted they did this. But they did not admit they had carved the thousands of other stones as well.

Now at this point a man less sure of himself would have hesitated. Most people would have at least considered the possibility that someone was fooling them. But not Dr. Beringer. He was absolutely sure he could not be fooled. He simply brushed aside Roderick and Eckart's charges.

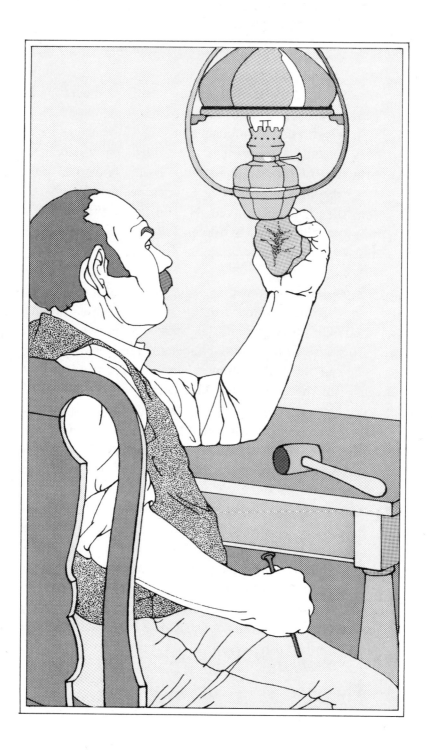

Beringer was so sure of himself that he wrote a book about the find. This book, he thought, would prove to the world that fossils were not the remains of dead creatures, but "sports of nature."

The book was published in 1726. It was large and very expensive to print. It contained many excellent drawings of the famous stones. In his book Dr. Beringer strongly defended his stones against the charge that they had been faked. He did admit that perhaps a few of the stones had been faked by Roderick and Eckart, but the vast majority, he said, were genuine beyond a doubt.

As soon as the book was published scholars all over Europe wanted a copy. Everyone was talking about Dr. Beringer and his amazing discoveries. But then a very strange thing happened. The book had only been out for a short time when Beringer tried to buy back all the copies that had been sold. He admitted that the stones were all frauds, and he had been fooled. His great book turned out to be a monument to his own error. Now he wanted to destroy every copy.

Why did Beringer change his mind after keeping it closed for so long? We don't really know. According to one story, he dug up a stone with his own name on it. Perhaps he just thought about the subject long enough to realize what had happened.

Whatever the reason, a lot of people who bought the book didn't want to sell it back. The price of the book actually went up. Later, after Beringer was dead, a new edition of the foolish work was issued. In the 1960s an English version of the book was published.

Beringer hoped that the book would make him famous. In a way it did. But not in the way that he had hoped or imagined.

Who were the hoaxers? An official inquiry was held into the case. Beringer's three young assistants who had found all the stones were carefully questioned. Two of them seem to have known nothing about the fraud. The third admitted that he had sold some false stones but said that he had never carved them himself.

But who did do the carving? Suspicion fell on Roderick and Eckart. They had both hated Dr. Beringer. They never seem to have actually been questioned, but Roderick left Würzburg shortly after the inquiry.

Beringer lived on for another fourteen years. He published two more books on other subjects. But no one took them seriously. His reputation as a scholar had been destroyed.

Today he is known as the classic example of a man so blinded by his own ideas that he cannot see what is very obvious to everyone else.

THE FLYING BOMB

The giant silvery airship turned to make its final approach. Two hundred feet over the field its powerful engines growled into reverse. The ship stopped and hovered motionless. Lines were dropped to the ground. The ground party rushed to pick them up.

That is how the giant zeppelin *Hindenburg* came

into Lakehurst, New Jersey, on the evening of May 6, 1937. Its arrival had been delayed for nearly ten hours by bad weather. But the weather had cleared, and the approach looked smooth and natural.

The *Hindenburg* had flown all the way from Germany. The trip had taken seventy-seven hours. Aboard were a total of ninety-seven passengers and crewmen. The *Hindenburg* was the fastest and most luxurious way to cross the Atlantic Ocean in 1937. It had already made ten crossings without a single mishap.

The giant zeppelin was still a novelty. Its arrival always made news. Among those waiting on the ground for the arrival were many photographers and radio men. One of the radio men was Herb Morrison of Station WLS. He was describing the moment for his listeners. He told them how gracefully the great silver ship glided in. Then suddenly his voice registered shock. "It's burst into flames!" he shouted into the microphone. "Oh my . . . it's burning, bursting into flames . . . Oh, the humanity and all the passengers." The radio announcer's voice broke into sobs. He couldn't go on.

That is how many people in America first learned that the *Hindenburg* had exploded and burned. Within less than forty seconds the entire ship was ablaze. People on the ground were stunned for a moment. Then they began to run for their lives, as the flaming giant crashed toward them. In a few terrible seconds thirty-five people had died as a result of the tragedy. Others were horribly burned or badly injured trying to jump to the ground. Remarkably, more than half of those aboard survived the disaster.

As a result of the *Hindenburg* explosion and fire zeppelin travel was completely abandoned. All remaining passenger-carrying zeppelins were grounded, permanently.

Airplanes were being developed in 1937. But they could not yet carry as many passengers as a zeppelin, and no passenger plane could fly the Atlantic. Ship crossings took days or weeks. But despite the comfort and speed of zeppelin travel, no one was willing to risk his life anymore.

Just exactly what caused the *Hindenburg* explosion no one knows. No one may ever know. Both the United States and Germany conducted investigations. Everybody who might possibly know anything about the explosion was interviewed. The official conclusions were that some sort of electrical spark had set off the explosion. No one could agree what caused the spark.

There were a lot of unofficial rumors as well. Some said that a bomb had caused the explosion. The Germans had been afraid of a bomb. Before the *Hindenburg* left Germany, all the passengers and crew had been searched carefully. The entire zeppelin was examined from top to bottom. No bomb was found. Still, two German air force officers rode along on the trip as a special precaution.

There are many theories about who might have planted a bomb and why. In 1937 Germany was firmly in control of Adolf Hitler's Nazi party. There were

a lot of people who had good reason to hate the Nazis.

The bomb theory is still discussed today. But no one has ever been able to find any solid evidence to support it. So the question of exactly what caused the *Hindenburg* explosion remains open.

But whatever started the explosion, everyone agrees that the real villain was hydrogen gas. Basically a zeppelin is a balloon. There is a motor that makes the ship go forward. But it is held up because it is lighter than air. The eight-hundred-foot long *Hindenburg* was filled with hydrogen gas. The inside of the ship contained sixteen gigantic bags or lifting cells containing a total of seven million cubic feet of hydrogen. Hydrogen is a gas that is lighter than air. It was the hydrogen that lifted the huge craft into the air. But hydrogen has one great drawback, it is highly flammable and explosive.

Zeppelins were not a new invention in 1937. They had been flown for years. The dangers of hydrogen gas were well known. There had already been several hydrogen-caused zeppelin disasters. There was a gas that could be used in place of hydrogen. Helium is another lighter-than-air gas, but it is not flammable and does not explode. Helium is the gas that is used to inflate the balloons that you buy at the zoo or a parade. It is quite safe to use.

In 1937 many zeppelins were already using helium. The *Hindenburg* itself had been built to use helium. But helium also has a drawback. It is expensive and hard to get compared to hydrogen. In 1937 there

100

was only one source for that much helium, the United States. To fill the *Hindenburg* with helium from the United States would have cost the Germans about $600,000. Besides, Hitler's Germany and the United States were not on the best of terms. The Germans thought that they could do without American helium.

The Germans were not the only country that had zeppelins, though they had pioneered in the development of this particular type of airship. Other countries also tried to develop their own zeppelins. For a while the United States had an ambitious zeppelin program. But most zeppelins were plagued with many different problems. Even the zeppelins that used non-explosive helium had problems. There were many crashes, and most countries, including the United States, either gave up zeppelin development or cut back on it.

The German zeppelins, however, worked beautifully. So the Germans began to think that no one else knew how to build or operate the giant ships. They also figured that hydrogen would not be dangerous if handled by experts, and they considered themselves the greatest experts in the world.

On May 6, 1937, over Lakehurst, New Jersey, they found out that they were wrong.

THE WRONG ENEMY

In 1492 Columbus was supposed to have proved the world is round. But as late as 1870 there were still people who refused to believe the world is round. One of them was an Englishman named John Hampden.

Hampden was sure the earth was as flat as a pan-

cake. In his view the North Pole was right in the center of the earth, and there was no South Pole. He believed the sun was quite small and was only seven hundred miles away from the flat earth.

Hampden was so sure the earth was flat that he offered to bet anyone £500 (about $2,500) that they could not prove the earth was round.

On January 12, 1870, Hampden printed his challenge in a scientific magazine.

When Alfred Russell Wallace read the challenge he could hardly believe his eyes. Here he thought, was a chance to put an end to all the flat-earth nonsense and make some money besides.

Wallace was a scientist. He had developed the theory of evolution at the same time as Charles Darwin. He was a very well-known man, and a real gentleman. But he made one big mistake, he thought John Hampden was a gentleman too. He wasn't, John Hampden was a fanatic.

Two judges were chosen to weigh the proof. Wallace appointed one, Hampden appointed the other. Wallace picked a man he thought would be fair. What Wallace did not know was that the man Hampden picked for judge was a flat-earther like himself.

Wallace decided to prove that the earth was round by conducting an experiment on a canal. Wallace placed a marker on two bridges six miles apart. Then he placed a marker halfway between the bridges. All the markers were exactly the same height from the surface of the canal. If you looked down the markers with a telescope, then you could actually see the curvature of the earth. Wallace's judge said that this was conclusive proof. Hampden's judge disagreed.

Wallace was amazed. The proof was so clear and simple, he could not understand how anyone could not be convinced. Hampden was not convinced at all. He started shouting that Wallace had lost the bet and should pay him. So a third judge was appointed. This judge was John Henry Walsh, a newspaper editor. Walsh studied the evidence, decided that Wallace had obviously won, and gave the money to him.

That should have been the end of it, but it wasn't. Hampden was enraged and demanded his money back. When he didn't get it he began writing and publishing pamphlets about Wallace and Walsh. He called them crooks, liars, fools, and worse.

At first Wallace tried to ignore Hampden. That just encouraged the fanatic to more furious efforts. There were more pamphlets, letters to the editor, and postcards to Wallace's friends and co-workers. Finally Wallace got tired of being called a crook, a liar, and a fool all the time. He sued Hampden. Wallace won the suit easily and was awarded £600 ($3,000). That was a very large sum. But Wallace couldn't collect. Hampden had already signed over all his money to a relative. Then when it came time to pay, he said he had no money. Wallace had to pay the lawyers himself.

Walsh also got tired of all the names he was being called. He had Hampden hauled into court too. This time Hampden was told to apologize and stop saying

all those terrible things, or he would be tossed into jail. Hampden apologized, but he didn't stop.

A few months later Hampden sent this letter to Mrs. Wallace.

Madame—if your infernal thief of a husband is brought home some day on a stretcher, with every bone in his head smashed to a pulp, you will know the reason. Do tell him from me he is a lying infernal thief, and as sure as his name is Wallace he never dies in his bed.

You must be a miserable wretch to be obliged to live with a convicted felon. Do not think or let him think I have done with him.

John Hampden.

That sounded very much like a threat. So Hampden was taken to court once again. He explained that he wasn't threatening anyone. It was only that some of his young friends were so angry about the way Wallace had treated him he thought they might hurt Wallace. Hampden said all he was trying to do was warn Wallace. No one believed that story. Hampden was sent to jail for a short time and made to promise that he would send no more letters. Hampden promised, but he didn't stop.

Over the next four years Wallace had Hampden in court three more times. Each time he was found guilty. The first time he got off by making another public apology. The next time he promised to print an apology in all the newspapers. But before he even got around to that he had already sent Wallace more furious letters. So Hampden was sent to prison for two months. As soon as he got out he started all over again. This time he was sentenced to a year in jail, but got out after only six months.

Now Hampden turned the tables. He sued to get his original £500 back. He claimed that it was a gambling debt, which in a way it was. The law did not recognize gambling debts as legal. Hampden didn't win that suit either, but Wallace got stuck for the legal costs again.

When Alfred Russell Wallace went over what had happened he realized how big a mistake he had made. He thought he was going to prove what he assumed nearly everybody believed anyway—that the world was round. And he would make a nice profit in the bargain. Instead he had spent years fighting off this fanatic, and it had cost him a good deal of money.

Hampden continued to bombard Wallace with letters and pamphlets. Wallace decided that the only thing he could do now was ignore the man, or try to. Finally, he even developed a sort of affection for his old rival. Still, he must have been relieved when John Hampden finally died on January 22, 1891.

Was Alfred Russell Wallace's long fight finally over? Perhaps not. By that time Wallace had become a spiritualist. That is, he believed that it was possible to talk to the spirits of people who had died. He may have feared that the fanatic John Hampden would come back from beyond the grave to denounce him.

There are a few flat-earthers even today. The International Flat Earth Research Society of America claims to have some 1,500 members.

One would think that pictures taken by satellites showing an obviously round earth would finish the flat-earthers once and for all. But people hang on to their beliefs, no matter how wrong they may be. When the first satellite picture of the whole earth was shown to the president of the British Flat Earth Society, he studied it for a moment. Then he said, "Yes, it's easy to see how this could fool the untrained eye." John Hampden would have said the same.

THE CHARGE OF THE LIGHT BRIGADE

Mistakes often happen in wars. One of the most spectacular and stupidest wartime mistakes took place at a spot called Balaklava in 1854.

Balaklava is in a part of Russia called the Crimea. The Crimea had been invaded by the British, French, and Turks. They wanted to capture a major Russian seaport called Sevastopol. The war became known as the Crimean War.

The reasons for the Crimean War are hard to understand. Today most historians believe the war was a mistake for everybody who was involved in it. But wars are much easier to start than they are to stop.

The main supply port for the British was Balaklava. It is located about six miles from Sevastopol. In order to defend the port the British and their allies had to control the high ground nearby. The first line of defense for Balaklava was in the hands of a small force of Turkish artillery men. If a Russian attack got past the artillery, it would then face the main British force.

British troops were commanded by Lord Raglan. The forces in the field consisted of a regiment of five hundred Highlanders under Sir Colin Campbell and two groups of cavalry under the overall command of Lord Lucan. The regiment of heavy cavalry, about nine hundred men, was led by General Sir James Scarlett. A smaller brigade of light cavalry was commanded by Lord Cardigan.

The Russians were trying desperately to choke off British supplies. They attacked Balaklava in force and swept past the Turks. The Russian troops then occupied some of the heights almost unopposed. They set up their own artillery.

A determined stand by the Highlanders stopped the Russian advance. A furious cavalry charge by Scarlett's Heavy Brigade drove the Russians back in confusion. If Cardigan's Light Brigade had joined the

attack, the battle might have ended right there. But for some reason Cardigan held his troops back.

From a distance Lord Raglan and his staff watched all of this. They were quite pleased with the way the battle was going. Then they saw that the Russians were getting ready to withdraw. They were going to take the captured Turkish cannons with them. Lord Raglan wanted to stop this. He issued an order that the Light Brigade should advance and stop the Russians from taking the cannons. However, Raglan's order was not entirely clear.

It was given first to Lord Lucan, who was the overall commander of the cavalry. From his position Lucan could not see the Turkish cannons. All he could see were Russian cannons. These had been placed on high ground at the other end of the valley. In order to get to those cannons the Light Brigade would have to charge right down the valley. On either side of the valley the hills were full of well-armed Russian troops. Any British troops in the middle of the valley would be easy targets for the Russians.

Lord Lucan knew that there must be something wrong with the order. He objected to it. But Lucan and Raglan had been feuding for a long time. They did not discuss the order to see what was wrong. The order was just repeated. So Lord Lucan sent it on to Lord Cardigan, who was to lead the charge.

Lord Cardigan also knew there was something wrong. He sent an objection to Lord Lucan. As it happened, Lord Lucan was also Lord Cardigan's brother-in-law. But that did not make them friends.

In fact, they greatly disliked one another. Instead of trying to find some way to get around this obviously mistaken order, Lord Lucan just repeated it.

Now it was up to Lord Cardigan. He could, of course, have refused to obey the order. Once matters were explained everyone would probably have understood. But Cardigan was an extremely proud and stubborn man. He had already fought duels to avenge what he thought were insults to his honor. He was afraid that someone might think he was a coward if he did not carry out orders. This was something he could not stand. So he gave the order to charge. And charge the Light Brigade did. They rode right down the valley with the Russians shooting at them from all sides.

Of the 673 men who began the charge, 113 were killed and another 134 were wounded or captured. There was a small French cavalry unit nearby. They saw what was happening, and attacked the Russians, to distract them. Otherwise things would have been even worse for the Light Brigade.

That was the end of the battle of Balaklava. The Russians had failed to capture the port. But the British had lost control of an important supply road. Generally the battle is considered a Russian victory. The battle really didn't make much difference. Within six weeks the Russians had abandoned the positions they captured. In the end the British and their allies won the Crimean War. They got very little out of the victory.

The charge of the Light Brigade was more than

a mistake. It was an act of sheer, blind stupidity. If the pig-headed commanders had talked to one another, it would never have taken place. But somehow the charge captured the imagination of the British public. There is no doubt that the men of the Light Brigade were brave. Every one of them knew the danger they faced. Yet when given the order to charge they never hesitated. They made a gallent attempt to do the impossible. What most people forgot was that the charge was not only impossible, but also entirely unnecessary.

Lord Cardigan had never been a very popular man. His arrogance and his temper had made people dislike him. But when he returned home from the Crimea he was a national hero. All the survivors of the Light Brigade were greeted as heroes.

The poet Alfred Lord Tennyson wrote a poem about the charge. One of the lines of the poem reads "Theirs not to reason why, theirs but to do and die." The poem is still popular in England today.

Somehow, people had managed to turn a horrible mistake into an inspiring victory.

THE CANALS OF MARS

Up to fifty years ago a lot of people had a very strange belief about the planet Mars. They thought the planet was crisscrossed by a network of canals. People could not agree as to what these canals were. Some thought they were natural features, cracks on the planet's surface.

Others disagreed. Those people said that the Martian canals were too straight and regular. They insisted that the canals had to be artificial features, that they were built by Martians.

On earth canals are used to carry water. Scientists knew that the surface of Mars had little if any water. Therefore, according to one theory, the canals must have been built thousands or hundreds of thousands of years ago. The canals had been used to help spread the planet's shrinking water supply. But finally, according to this theory, all the water was gone. The Martian civilization died out. Only the vast network of empty canals remained as evidence that a Martian civilization had ever existed.

That is an attractive story. At one time a lot of people believed it, including some very well-known astronomers. But we now know, beyond a shadow of a doubt, that the story is wrong. In fact, there are no canals of any kind on Mars. There never have been. There probably have never been any Martians either. How and why did this very strange idea get started?

We know when and where the idea started, but we are not sure how or why.

Astronomers had been observing the surface of Mars through telescopes for a long time. Then in 1877, the Italian astronomer G. V. Schiaparelli saw something on the planet no one else had ever reported. He saw streaks across the planet's surface.

Other observers had looked at Mars through better telescopes. But Schiaparelli was viewing the planet under unusually favorable conditions, Schiaparelli was

known as a careful astronomer. His observation was taken seriously.

Schiaparelli called the streaks *canali*. That is an Italian word that means channels. A channel is not necessarily something artificial. But when Schiaparelli's *canali* was translated into English it came out canals. Immediately everybody thought of earthly canals, which are man-made.

The canals of Mars were not accepted by scientists at once. But soon other astronomers reported seeing them. They made many different maps of these canals.

The biggest supporter of the Martian canals was the American astronomer Percival Lowell. Lowell was one of the world's leading astronomers. What is more, he was director of the observatory at Flagstaff, Arizona. The Flagstaff Observatory was the finest observatory in the world. When Lowell looked through his telescope he should have been able to see Mars more clearly than anyone else in the world. And when Lowell looked through his telescope he saw canals on Mars, lots of them.

To Percival Lowell's eye the surface of Mars was covered by a spiderweb of absolutely straight canals. At the points where one canal crossed another Lowell saw a dark spot. He called all such spots an oasis.

Lowell was convinced that the canals were of artificial origin. He said that they were built by Martians. The purpose of the canals, according to Lowell, was to bring water from the melting polar ice caps, to the rest of the dry planet. The water would be used to irrigate the Martian crops.

Some astronomers supported Lowell's theory. Others believed in the canals, but doubted that they were of artificial origin. Still others said there were no canals at all. This last group was not being stubborn. They looked through their telescopes and didn't see any canals.

At best the canals were very faint. A small difference in the type of telescope or in atmospheric conditions made Mars look different. So the controversy continued.

You might think that photographs of Mars would settle the question. But in those days photographs of planets were not very good. Photos didn't show any canals. But astronomers could see more by looking directly through the telescope than by taking photos.

Lowell remained an ardent supporter of the canal idea until his death in 1916. After that the whole canal controversy began to die down. This was mainly because fewer and fewer astronomers reported seeing the canals.

Still, for many years occasional sightings of the Martian canals were reported, but fewer and fewer people believed in them.

The whole canal controversy was not finally settled until space probes were sent near Mars in the 1970s. The photographs sent back from these probes gave scientists a much closer look at the planet than was possible with earthbound telescopes. These photos showed no canals.

The surface of Mars is covered with craters, like the surface of the moon. There are cracks in the Martian surface. There are also the remains of what might once have been rivers. So there could have been water on Mars, though there is little or none today. But neither the cracks nor the possible dry riverbeds can account for the Martian canals. These features are far too faint to have been seen by Schiaparelli, Lowell, and others.

Then what were the "canals" of Mars? No one really knows. They were probably some sort of optical illusion. The illusion would have been strengthened by what an observer expected to see. People who believed in the canals of Mars were more likely to see them.

THE SPY WHO WOULD NOT DIE

On Tuesday, May 3, 1960, a small article appeared in many American newspapers. It said that a U.S. weather research plane based in Turkey had been lost. The story went on to say the plane had disappeared somewhere near the border between Iran and the Soviet Union.

During the next few days the little story grew and grew. It became one of the biggest spy scandals in U.S. history.

The time, May 1960, was important. For years the United States and the Soviet Union had been bitterly hostile to one another. The two countries were barely speaking. When they did say something it was usually a threat. This was the period known as the cold war. People all over the world were scared. They feared that the cold war could become a real hot war at any moment. Both the United States and the Soviets had nuclear missiles pointed at one another.

But by 1960 the relations between the United States and the Soviets got a little better. President Dwight Eisenhower and Soviet Leader Nikita Khrushchev were supposed to meet in Paris. It was to be the first official meeting of the leaders of the two countries in many years. No one expected any miracles, but at least it seemed as if war were a little further off.

Then came that story about the weather plane.

The Soviets said that the plane was not a weather plane at all. They said it was a spy plane. The purpose of the plane, according to the Soviets, was to fly over their country and take pictures of Soviet missiles. President Eisenhower personally denied this. He said that the missing plane was no spy plane.

Then the Soviets surprised everybody. They produced the plane and the pilot. The pilot, a man named Francis Gary Powers, was not only alive, but also talking. The plane was loaded with spy equipment. It had been shot down or crashed deep in Soviet territory.

Powers admitted that he was spying. He said that he worked for the Central Intelligence Agency, or C.I.A., the U.S. spy agency. The president of the United States had been caught in a flat lie. He was forced to admit he had lied. Both the president himself and the entire country were deeply embarrassed.

The meeting between the leaders of the United States and the Soviet Union was called off. There was much hard feeling on both sides. The world was plunged right back into the cold war.

In one way the situation was not as serious as it looked. The Soviets were not surprised the United States was using spy planes. They knew this sort of spying was going on, and they had been complaining about it for years. The Soviets did their own spying in the United States.

But the United States never openly admitted that it spied. Neither did the Soviets. It is one thing to know others are spying on you, quite another to catch a spy red-handed. It is even worse for a world leader to get trapped in an obvious lie.

How had all this come about? It was all a mistake, or rather a series of mistakes. The first mistake was the timing of the flight. It took place on May 1, May Day, the most important holiday in the Soviet Union. How would Americans have felt if a Soviet spy plane crashed near Chicago on July 4?

The flight came right before the scheduled meeting of United States and Soviet leaders. It was also the longest and, therefore, most dangerous of these spy flights ever attempted. The C.I.A. may have been trying to gather all possible information on Soviet missiles before the meeting. They gambled on the long flight—and lost.

It was also a mistake to assume that the plane would not be shot down or crash. To this day no one seems sure whether the plane was hit by a Soviet missile or suffered some kind of mechanical failure. The plane, called a U-2, was able to fly at exceptionally high altitudes. The United States believed that it would remain out of range of Soviet missiles.

If the plane was shot down or crashed, however, then the C.I.A. was absolutely sure that the plane itself would be destroyed and the pilot killed. If that had happened, the story about the weather plane would have held. No one would have believed it, but no one could have proved it was wrong. Powers, however, was able to parachute to safety. The plane itself was in surprisingly good shape after the crash. The Soviets put it on display in a Moscow park.

Was the U-2 pilot supposed to blow up the plane and then kill himself in case of emergency? An explosive package was found aboard the plane. Powers carried a poison needle. The C.I.A. insisted that Powers had never been ordered to kill himself. The explosives were only to blow up secret materials on the plane, not the whole plane, pilot and all. Powers said he had not been able to reach the button that set off the explosives. The poison was only in case he was captured and tortured, or badly injured and beyond help.

Powers said that he was never told what he should

do if he was captured, because no one ever thought a U-2 pilot would be captured. It was, he said, "a bad mistake."

Francis Gary Powers was brought to trial in Moscow. His trial was open and quite fair by Soviet standards. The U-2 pilot admitted that he had been spying and said he was sorry. He was given a ten-year sentence. In the past the Soviets had shot captured spies.

Powers never served his full sentence. Two years after he was sent to prison he was exchanged for a Soviet spy captured in the United States.

When Powers got back to the United States there was no hero's welcome for him. No one actually came out and said that he should have killed himself, but a lot of people seemed to think that he should have. The U.S. government investigated the whole case. They finally concluded that Powers had done nothing wrong. Later the C.I.A. gave him an award. He resigned from the C.I.A., anyway, and was bitter about how he had been treated.

All the details of this case are not known. They never are in spy cases. But one thing is clear—there was no real plan to deal with the possibility that a U-2 would crash or be shot down and its pilot captured alive. Everybody in the C.I.A. assumed that could never happen. Everybody in the C.I.A. was wrong.

THE TRIPLE DOUBLE PLAY

Professional baseball players, like everyone else in the world, make their share of mistakes. Some players make more than their share. One such player was Floyd "Babe" Herman, who played for the old Brooklyn Dodgers.

Herman was the sort of player known as "good hit,

no field." Many power hitters have been poor fielders. But not only was Babe exceptionally bad, but he almost took pride in his poor performance. He played for the Dodgers during the 1920s and 1930s. At that time the team was known for its zaniness, and Babe Herman was the zaniest Dodger of them all.

When he had been in the minor leagues Babe had once been thrown off a team. This happened after the team owner saw him get hit on the head while trying to catch a simple fly ball.

The team manager objected. "I can't fire him. He's leading the league in hitting with four-sixteen."

"I don't care if he's hitting four thousand," said the owner. "I'm not going to have players who field the ball with their skulls."

Herman made it to the majors anyway, where he regularly hit over .300. But his fielding hadn't improved a bit. He led the league in outfield errors three straight years. Four other years he came close.

In addition to being a poor fielder, Herman was also a clown. The sports reporters loved him. He was a lot of fun to write about. One year one of the reporters offered to bet Herman that he would be hit on the head by a fly ball before the season ended. Herman acted as if his dignity was offended. "I'm not as bad a fielder as you guys think," he said. "I'll take the bet."

As the reporter and the baseball player were shaking on the bet Herman had second thoughts. "On the shoulder don't count," he said.

The fans loved Babe Herman too. In fact, they

loved the whole Brooklyn team. And it took some co-operation from his teammates to allow Babe Herman to pull off his famous classic mistake.

If Babe Herman's fielding was bad, his base running was even worse. He would run head-down, paying no attention to what might be happening anywhere else.

The situation was this: The bases were full of Dodgers. Hank DeBerry, the catcher, was on third. Dazzy Vance, a blazing fastball pitcher, and a zany in his own right, was on second. Chick Fewster, an outfielder, was on first. There was one out and Babe Herman stepped up to bat.

He hit a tremendous blast against the outfield wall. It was an easy double, perhaps even a triple. DeBerry scored without any trouble. Vance didn't like to run very much. He thought the ball might be caught and the running would be wasted effort. So he hesitated between second and third. When the ball hit the wall he ran past third, but then figured he couldn't score so headed back. Fewster, who had been right behind Vance, now turned around and ran back toward second.

Herman, who had made the hit, was unaware of what was going on with his teammates. He was running in his usual head-down fashion. He rounded second and passed Fewster, who was running back to base. If one runner passes another on the base paths, he is automatically out. But that happens so rarely that no one, except the umpire, seemed aware of it. He motioned that Herman was out. Herman didn't see the umpire's sign and slid into third, just as Vance was sliding in from the opposite direction.

The ball arrived at about the same time. The third basemen didn't know what to do. He tagged Herman, who was already out, and then tagged Vance, who was standing safely on the base.

Fewster should have run back to second, where he would have been safe. But somehow being passed by Herman seemed to confuse him. He just stood there and watched the drama at third.

Finally the third basemen discovered that there were still only two Brooklyn outs. There was Fewster standing between second and third. The third basemen decided to run him down. Fewster ran back to second. But instead of stopping there, where he would have been safe, he kept right on running. The third basemen finally caught up with him in the outfield, and tagged him for the third out. And that's how Babe Herman tripled into a double play. No professional baseball player has ever duplicated that feat.

The only man who ever came close was Babe Herman himself. In a somewhat similar situation Herman came up to bat with a man on first. He hit a hard line smash and headed head-down for first. The man on first headed for second. But then he feared that the ball was going to be caught and he would be out. So he stopped and ran back toward first. In the meantime, Herman had already reached first and was on his way to second. The two teammates passed each other on the base paths.

That sort of base running led to a classic baseball

story. A Brooklyn fan was late for a game. He was hurrying up the ramp at old Ebbets Field. He yelled up to somebody in the grandstand, "What's happening?"

The man replied, "The Brooks got three on."

"Yeah," said the latecomer, "which base."

THE SPRUCE GOOSE

Howard Hughes was a very rich man. He was also a very strange man. Before he died in 1977 he had not been seen in public for years. But Howard Hughes had not hidden away all of his life.

True, Hughes had never cared for publicity. But at one time he did not go to any great lengths to avoid it either. He went to Hollywood and produced movies. He even married a well-known movie star.

Movies were only a sideline for Hughes. What he was really interested in was airplanes. He had become quite famous as an airplane builder and pilot.

Some people said that Howard Hughes knew more about airplanes than anyone else in the world. But Hughes made one big and very expensive airplane mistake—it was called the Spruce Goose.

The project started during World War II. Americans had to send a lot of supplies overseas. But sending cargo ships across the ocean was costly and dangerous. Many ships were sunk by enemy submarines. A millionaire shipbuilder named Henry J. Kaiser had an idea: If ships couldn't do the job perhaps huge cargo planes could.

Kaiser knew a lot about ships, but he didn't know much about airplanes. So he got his fellow millionaire Howard Hughes interested in the project. Soon Kaiser dropped out of the project. Building the huge cargo plane was entirely in the hands of Howard Hughes. The plane was described as a flying boat. It was to take off and land in the water.

The U.S. government agreed to pay for building three of the giant planes. But the project was in trouble even before it got started.

In addition to building ships, Henry J. Kaiser owned an aluminum company. During wartime all metals were scarce. Kaiser had boasted that he could easily get enough aluminum for the planes. Hughes soon found out that Kaiser couldn't get the aluminum.

Neither could anyone else. In fact there were no metals easily available. The only building materials that Hughes could get for the gigantic building project were wood and plastic. So Hughes decided to build his flying boat out of wood and plastic.

Officially the flying boat was to be called *Hercules*. Very few ever called it that. Unofficially it became known as the "Flying Lumberyard," the "Flying Coffin," and most commonly, the "Spruce Goose." Hughes hated that name. He became very angry whenever anyone referred to his plane as the Spruce Goose. But pople did it anyway.

Kaiser had promised that the three planes would be completed within ten months. Very few took that kind of a deadline seriously. People who know the difficulties of building aircraft figured that the planes might be ready for testing in about two years. But it soon became obvious that even that extended deadline was not going to be met. And the plane was going to be a lot more expensive than anyone had bargained for.

There were many reasons for the problems. The sheer size of the plane was one. No one had ever attempted to build anything like it before. Then there were delays and confusion with the government contracts. When Kaiser dropped out, he took all of his engineers with him. This caused more confusion.

But a major source of the problem was Howard Hughes himself. He was already showing distinct signs of the strangeness that was to turn him into a complete recluse in his later life. He was a perfectionist. He had to approve every single nut and bolt personally. Hughes was a hard worker, but that was too big a job for any single person.

Getting Howard Hughes to approve something wasn't easy. Often days or weeks went by when no one could get in touch with him. He hated meetings. Often he would call people up in the middle of the night to get information.

The building of the giant plane went on, but ever so slowly. The original plan called for three planes at a cost of $13.5 million. Two years later it was clear that there was only going to be one plane and the cost would be over $20 million. And no one had any idea when the thing would be finished, or what it would finally cost.

Some people in the government wanted to drop the whole project. But Howard Hughes was a powerful man. The government was persuaded to renew the contract. So the building of the Spruce Goose continued, with no end in sight. However, World War II did end. Other forms of aircraft were developed. Even if the Spruce Goose were finished, it would no longer be needed.

Hughes's giant plane became something of a mystery. It was being built in a huge and closely guarded hangar in California. Very few people had been allowed to see it. No one was sure that even if it were finished that it would fly.

By 1947 some members of the U.S. Senate were

fed up with Howard Hughes and the Spruce Goose. They thought that the U.S. government had been cheated and the plane would never fly.

That made Hughes very angry. He insisted his plane would fly, and he was going to prove it. In November 1947 Hughes invited the senators, reporters, and a lot of other people to watch the test of the plane. It was to be held in the ocean off Long Beach, California. Hughes himself was going to fly the plane.

When the visitors caught their first sight of the Spruce Goose they were impressed. It had a wingspan of 320 feet—longer than a football field. It was 200 feet long, was powered by eight engines, and it was made of wood. They had never seen anything like it. But would it fly? That was the big question.

On the day of the test a large crowd gathered on the beach. But the weather was not very good and the test was canceled. The next day the weather was not any better. Hughes was impatient. He decided to run the test anyway. But he said that it would be short and at a low speed. He said that he was not going to risk taking off this day. He was just going to taxi along the water.

After making that announcement Hughes did just the opposite. He sped down the water at one hundred miles per hour. The plane reached takeoff speed. It shook, and then it rose slowly into the air. It reached an altitude of about seventy feet, and flew for about a mile. Then Hughes gently lowered it back into the sea.

The thing could fly. People on the shore cheered. At a news conference afterward, Hughes seemed very happy. It was a great triumph. Some people even suggested that Howard Hughes should run for president.

After the test the Spruce Goose was taken back to its hangar. But there were no more tests. Was Howard Hughes still working on it? No one seemed to know. The plane was never taken out of its hangar again. It is still there today.

What happened? Why had Howard Hughes hidden the Spruce Goose after its apparently successful test? No one knows for sure. Hughes never explained anything. But after he died some people who knew him said Hughes never tested the plane again because he was afraid. During that November 1947 test the plane shook so badly he thought it would fall apart. He knew the plane would never be any good, but refused to admit it.

Whatever the reasons, no one can doubt that the Spruce Goose was a very large, very expensive mistake.

INDEX